KT-116-579

Who is Jesus?

Roger Carswell

CHRISTIAN FOCUS

Roger Carswell worked as a secondary schoolteacher in West Yorkshire for over ten years. He now works full-time speaking around the world to students and adults about the believability of the Christian faith and its relevance to modern life. His other books include *And Some Evangelists* (ISBN 978-1-85792-512-8) and *Things God Wants Us to Know* (ISBN 978-1-84550-242-3). He is married to Dot and they have four children.

Unless otherwise indicated, all Scripture quotations are taken from the Holy Bible, New Living Translation, NLT copyright © 1996. Used by permission of Tyndale House Publishers, Inc., Wheaton, Illinois 60189. All rights reserved.

Scripture quotations marked 'NIV' are taken from the HOLY BIBLE, NEW INTERNATIONAL VERSION. Copyright © 1973, 1978, 1984 by International Bible Society. Used by permission of Hodder & Stoughton Publishers, A member of the Hodder Headline Group. All rights reserved. 'NIV' is a registered trademark of International Bible Society. UK trademark number 1448790.

Scripture quotations marked 'NKJV' are taken from the New King James Version. Copyright © 1982 by Thomas Nelson, Inc. Used by permission. All rights reserved.

ISBN 978-1-84550-635-3

© Roger Carswell

10 9 8 7 6 5 4 3 2 1

Published in 2011
by
Christian Focus Publications, Ltd.,
Geanies House, Fearn, Ross-shire,
IV20 1TW, Great Britain.

www.christianfocus.com

Cover design by Moose77.com

Printed by
 Grafica Veneta

Mixed Sources
Product group from well-managed forests and other controlled sources
www.fsc.org Cert no. TT-COC-002769
© 1996 Forest Stewardship Council

Contents

Dedication

This book is dedicated
to

My six grandsons

who have brought me joy more than they can
imagine. Harry, Noah, Theo, Seth, Bo and Samuel.
I pray that you would trust, love and follow Jesus
and find Him to be altogether lovely.

Foreword

I became a Christian at the age of fifteen while on holiday in Lebanon, staying with my relatives who ran a Christian hospital in Beirut. I had had a wonderful holiday, but towards the end of my month there my uncle, Hagop Sagharian, spoke with me about Jesus. I had just beaten him at tennis – but then he was three times my age – but he was about to impact me in a way that would change me for ever.

Using a pocket Bible, he showed me short passages outlining the gospel. He spoke to me about God, explained that the Bible said I was guilty of sin, but that Jesus had come into the world with the express purpose of dying to pay the penalty for my wrong.

He showed me how Jesus had risen from the dead, but it was his explanation of the death of Jesus which struck home to me. When I understood that Jesus had paid the penalty for my sin, and had done so because of His love for me, I felt I had to trust Him as my Lord, Saviour and Friend.

That decision was like a hinge which changed the whole direction of my life. My interests and involvements are many, but what defines me is simply Jesus. He means everything to me. Since becoming a Christian, nothing has ever happened that has dulled my love for Him. And this little book is commending Him to you. Nothing would give me more pleasure than to hear that you too have come to know Him who said that He had come to give life, and give it more abundantly.

I want to thank those who have read, criticized and improved my manuscript. I am grateful to Mrs Jean Smith of Leicester, Ossie Ross of Long Crendon and Ben Carswell for their constructive and always helpful input.

Roger Carswell
January 2011

One

Introducing Jesus

He is easily the dominant figure in history … A historian without any theological bias whatever should find that he simply cannot portray the progress of humanity honestly without giving a foremost place to the teacher from Nazareth.

H.G. Wells
author

Towering above the rest of humanity stands one Man whose life, death and influence have had a greater impact than any other. For 2,000 years men and women have travelled the world to make this Man known. Millions today esteem, trust and follow Him, not because of compulsion but out of love. His life has never been equalled.

I would love to know what Jesus looked like, to hear His voice, to eavesdrop as He gave thanks before a meal, to watch Him as He spoke to children, or even see Him playing as a child, but we don't have these details. In reality, they are not important. But who He is and what

He accomplished in His life, death and resurrection are of utmost importance. According to the Bible, it is how we respond to Him that will determine our whole eternity.

We know that when John, the disciple who had been with Jesus for three years but was now imprisoned on the Isle of Patmos in the Mediterranean Sea, had a revelation of Jesus in heaven, he fell down at His feet as dead.[1] Jesus is startling as a person, amazing in His grace, tender in His compassion and love, whilst being unequalled in His authority and power.

Jesus was born in the little village of Bethlehem, eight miles south of Jerusalem. He was the son of a young peasant woman. He grew up in Nazareth to the north (I like to think He had a northern accent!), where He worked in a carpenter's shop until He was thirty. Then for three years He became a travelling preacher. He never wrote a book. He didn't compose any songs. He never married or had a family, or owned a house. He didn't go to college. He never visited a big city except, of course, Jerusalem. He never travelled more than 200 miles from the place where He was born. He did none of those things one usually associates with greatness.

He had no credentials but Himself. He owned nothing but His robe. He once said that foxes have holes in the ground and birds have nests, but He, the Son of Man, had nowhere even to lay His head. He preached from a borrowed boat and had to borrow a coin when

He made the point that we are to render to Caesar the things which are Caesar's and to God the things that are God's. He rode to Jerusalem on a borrowed ass, and was eventually buried in a borrowed tomb.

He was only thirty-three when the tide of public opinion turned against Him. His friends ran away. They once forsook everything to follow Him, but now they forsook Him and fled. One denied even knowing Him. Another sold Him for the price of a slave. He was turned over to His enemies and went through a mockery of a trial. He was executed by the state. While He was being executed, His executioners gambled for His clothing, the only property He had on earth. When He was dead, He was laid in a grave donated through the pity of a friend.

Twenty centuries have come and gone, and today He is still the central figure of the human race and all history. All the armies that ever marched, all the navies that ever sailed, all the parliaments that ever sat, all the kings that ever reigned, put together, have not affected the life of human beings on this earth as much as Jesus.[2]

Jesus' impact on the world has been immense. All types of people have tried to claim Him as their own, describing Him as a revolutionary, a hippie, a feminist, a Communist, and even the partner of Mary Magdalene and father of her children! In a perverse way though, His name is just a word of blasphemy for many, even that speaks of His significance. We don't curse using the name of any other religious or even political leader. The Bible has hundreds of names for Jesus, but supremely He is called Prophet, Priest, King, Messiah and Lord.

Books by their thousands have been written about Him, and even more because of Him. His life and death have been the backcloth drama of so many of our classics such as *A Tale of Two Cities* where the innocent dies in place of the guilty, or *The Pilgrim's Progress*, *Robinson Crusoe, Coral Island* or *Uncle Tom's Cabin*. William Shakespeare, writing nearly 500 years ago, captures the significance of Jesus in his play, *Henry IV*:

> Those holy fields
> Over whose acres walk'd those blessed feet
> Which, fourteen hundred years ago, were nail'd
> For our advantage on the bitter cross.

His mark on music has been immense, whether Bach's *Jesu, Joy of Man's Desiring*, Handel's *Messiah* or Andrew Lloyd Webber's *Jesus Christ Superstar*. Tens of thousands of hymns have been written in His praise, many of which are part of our Western culture and heritage – think of 'Amazing Grace' and 'The Old Rugged Cross'.

To visit any art gallery in the world is to be impressed again as to how Jesus has been the subject of thousands of artists who are struck by His birth, His life, His death and His resurrection. Artists have depicted Jesus as a baby, as a child and in His ministry. He has been painted with animals, children, His disciples, as well as with lepers and outcasts, or before Pilate, and, of course, hanging on the cross. He is the most painted person of all time.

Architecture has been impacted by Jesus. Buildings built for the glory of God and the worship of Jesus are amongst the greatest structures in the world. Bill Bryson described Durham Cathedral, which was built without an architect, as the greatest building in the northern hemisphere, and that led to him being made chancellor of Durham University! Churches, chapels and cathedrals have been designed so that their worship can exalt Jesus.

It is because of Jesus that His followers have built hospitals and schools, and worked for an acceptable standard in prisons. Jesus said that those who belong to Him will give food to the hungry and drink to the thirsty; they will care for strangers, clothe the naked, as well as visit the sick and prisoners. Social reformers like William Wilberforce, who worked tirelessly for the abolition of slavery, Lord Shaftesbury, 'the poor man's earl', who fought for the abolition of child labour, Elizabeth Fry and John Howard, who strove to bring about prison reform, and Florence Nightingale who cared for the wounded in the Crimean War, did so because they were followers of Jesus. Thomas Barnardo and George Müller began their orphanages because, as

Christians, they had a concern for orphaned children, and a desire to see them helped for the glory of God.

In recent years, Christians have been at the forefront of campaigns such as 'Stop the Traffik', caring for street children in South America, India and the Far East, as well as running drug rehabilitation centres and numerous aid agencies in needy parts of the world.

Whereas we are sometimes told to practise what we preach, Jesus preached what He had practised. His standard of morality has never been surpassed, yet He only taught us what He was doing. He loved His enemies; He prayed for those who persecuted Him; He went the extra mile; He cared for the underdog; He was the Friend of sinners, and He loved us and gave Himself for us on the cross. He never needed to apologize, or blush with embarrassment or shame. There was no duplicity or sham in the life of Jesus. He didn't pander to the whims of the influential to seek their favour. He reached out to the underdogs of society. He sought to benefit the outcasts. Children loved to be near Him; the worldly-wise could not trap Him with their trick question but were confounded by His wisdom.

There have been many famous deaths in history. From the death of Socrates to Joan of Arc to Nelson on the quarterdeck, and more recently Marilyn Monroe, J. F. Kennedy, Diana, Princess of Wales, and Michael Jackson – they have each left their mark on history. But no death has made such an impact as that of Jesus on the cross.

Thousands died by crucifixion, but Jesus' death has become the centre point of Christianity. It is at the cross that God made a way back to Himself from our waywardness.

Yet history records that Jesus not only died but was buried and three days later rose from the dead. I have a friend who used to be a schoolteacher. On one occasion, he took a group of pupils to the centre of London on a day trip. As part of the trip they visited Madame Tussaud's. As the students wandered around, he was leaning against a pillar in the Chamber of Horrors, when a small group of people gathered around him mistaking him for one of the waxwork models. They tried to discover what number he was and to identify him in their catalogue. He savoured the moment, but soon couldn't help smiling. The crowd realized their mistake and quickly went away. For a moment they thought he was a figure of history, only to discover he was really a living person.[3] Jesus was both.

So who is Jesus? When Jesus was walking with His twelve disciples near Caesarea Philippi, He asked them that question, 'Who do men say that I am?'[4] The disciples gave various answers, but then Jesus put His finger on the nerve when He asked, 'But who do you say that I am?'

There is no more important question to answer. Our answer will determine our eternal destiny. So, who is Jesus? In the following chapters, we will look at four answers, examining Jesus from different angles.

ENDNOTES

1. I, John, am your brother and your partner in suffering and in God's Kingdom and in the patient endurance to which Jesus calls us. I was exiled to the island of Patmos for preaching the word of God and for my testimony about Jesus. It was the Lord's Day, and I was worshipping in the Spirit. Suddenly, I heard behind me a loud voice like a trumpet blast …

   When I turned to see who was speaking to me, I saw seven gold lampstands. And standing in the middle of the lampstands was someone like the Son of Man. He was wearing a long robe with a gold sash across his chest. His head and His hair were white like wool, as white as snow.

   His eyes were like flames of fire. His feet were like polished bronze refined in a furnace, and His voice thundered like mighty ocean waves. He held seven stars in His right hand, and a sharp two-edged sword came from His mouth. And His face was like the sun in all its brilliance.

   When I saw Him, I fell at His feet as if I were dead. But He laid His right hand on me and said, "Don't be afraid! I am the First and the Last. I am the living one. I died, but look—I am alive forever and ever! And I hold the keys of death and the grave."(Rev. 1:9-18)

2. The preceding four paragraphs have been adapted from an article 'One Solitary Life' from James Allen Francis' work *The Real Jesus and Other Sermons*, 1926, Judson Press of Philadelphia, pp. 123-4.

3. Taken from the booklet *The best news in the world* by David Fletcher, available from St Ebbe's Church, Oxford.

4. Mark 8:27-31.

Two

He is the man of God
... and we should receive Him

Remember, Christ was not a deified man; neither was He a humanised God. He was perfectly God and at the same time perfectly man.

Charles Haddon Spurgeon
19th-century preacher

irst, let it be said that Jesus is a real man of history. He really did live, but His life is without parallel. In every way His is a remarkable life. Consider this: His biography was written before He was born! Old Testament prophets, writing hundred of years before Jesus' birth, were announcing that the Messiah would come and were telling us all about Him. They told us that:

* He would be born of a virgin.[1]
* He would be born in Bethlehem.[2]
* He would be called Lord.[3]

- He would be preceded by a messenger. [4]
- He would perform miracles. [5]
- He would teach in parables. [6]
- He would be betrayed by a friend. [7]
- He would be sold for thirty pieces of silver. [8]
- He would be forsaken by His disciples. [9]
- He would be silent before His accusers. [10]
- He would be smitten and spat upon. [11]
- He would be mocked. [12]
- His hands and His feet would be pierced. [13]
- He would be crucified with thieves. [14]
- He would pray for His persecutors. [15]
- He would be rejected by His own people. [16]
- He would be hated without a reason. [17]
- They would gamble for His garments. [18]
- He would suffer thirst, and be offered gall and vinegar. [19]
- His bones would not be broken. [20]
- His side would be pierced. [21]
- There would be darkness over all the land. [22]
- He would be buried in a rich man's tomb. [23]
- He would rise again from the dead. [24]
- He would ascend to heaven. [25]
- His influence would spread continually. [26]

All these, and many more not listed here, were fulfilled in the one solitary life of Jesus.

We have the record of Christian writers such as Matthew, Mark, Luke and John, as well as others whose writings are not contained in our New Testament. There are also Roman[27] and Jewish[28] historians of the same period in history as Jesus and His early followers, who testify to the historicity of Jesus. No serious historian has doubted this.

People have thrown up some strange ideas about who Jesus really is. In a more superstitious past some have suggested that He was an angel or mystical character far removed from our mundane human existence.

However, as one reads the four Gospels, which describe the life of Jesus, it is very clear that He was fully human. He was as much a man as any man is a man! Jesus was part of a human family. Mary was His mother. We read little of Joseph who married Mary, but we know that Jesus had brothers and sisters, four of whom are named in the Bible.[29] Jesus was at ease socializing and partying. His first miracle (changing water into wine) was done at the wedding of two of His friends at Cana in Galilee. He was perfectly at home celebrating and even feasting. When Matthew, the corrupt tax collector, left his work to follow Jesus, we find Jesus the centre of attention at the feast which followed. In fact, Jesus likened the kingdom of God to attending a banquet.

Prophesying 700 years before His birth, the Bible said: 'For unto us a Child is born, unto us a Son is given, and the government will be upon His shoulder. And His name will be called Wonderful, Counsellor, Mighty God, Everlasting Father, Prince of Peace. Of the increase of His government and peace there will be no end ...'[30]

John the disciple wrote: 'In the beginning was the Word, and the Word was with God, and the Word was God … and the Word was made flesh and made His dwelling among us.'[31]

God was big enough to become small, and strong enough to become weak – as weak as a tiny little foetus implanted into a virgin mother's womb. Jesus is the God-Man. The baby, who was laid in a manger in Bethlehem, was God coming into our world. The Creator became like us, His creation. He clothed Himself with a human body. God was encased in human flesh and bones. Religious cults that have sprung out of America, as well as world religions such as Islam and others, are keen to say that Jesus could not be both fully God and fully human, but it is what Jesus claimed for Himself and demonstrated in all that He did.

As a man, Jesus knew what it was to be tempted with the issues that we still find so alluring. The Bible says of Jesus that He was tempted in all points as are we, yet He was without sin. Imagine, Jesus knew what it was to be drawn to steal, to kill, to lust, to lie, to be jealous, to be spiteful, to swear, and a million other sins which characterize our lives. He never succumbed, as He was absolutely without sin. It is hard for us to imagine this Man who was intrinsically pure and clean.

Jesus at times was physically exhausted and emotionally drained. He slept in the back of a boat even though it was being thrown around by a storm at sea. He needed times alone to be able to pray and commune with His Father God. It hurt Him when one of His twelve disciples, Judas, betrayed Him for thirty pieces of silver, even though Jesus knew that this would happen. He grieved that people whom He loved rejected Him and eventually cried out for Him to be crucified. When a rich, young ruler turned his back on Jesus because the cost of following Him was too great, it pained Him.

Jesus experienced hunger and thirst. He worked hard, as a servant of His Father and then of those around Him, as He sought to meet their needs. He was available to all. He said of Himself that He came not to be served, but to serve and give Himself as a ransom for many. Ordinary people loved to hear Him and be near Him.

In the 2010 General Election in the UK there was a terrible moment for the incumbent Prime Minister, Gordon Brown, which became a defining point in his campaign to be re-elected. Having met an old-age pensioner from Rochdale in Lancashire and spoken courteously to her, thinking he was no longer miked up, he cuttingly called 'that woman' a 'bigot'. All credit to him, embarrassed and ashamed, he went back to her to apologize, but there was nothing like that in Jesus. He genuinely loved all people and wanted them to be part of the kingdom of Heaven.

There were occasions in Jesus' three years of ministry where the disciples felt that He needed peace and quiet. So, meaning well, they tried to protect Jesus, believing He needed space for Himself. But whether it was a hungry crowd of people pressing in on Him, or a grieving widow weeping over the death of her only son, or just a throng of children, Jesus made Himself available to them.

Jesus' teaching has never been surpassed. He did not sweeten His message to earn favours. This is how He described us as people who dared to defy God: 'It is what comes from inside that defiles you. For from within, out of a person's heart, come evil thoughts, sexual immorality, theft, murder, adultery, greed, wickedness, deceit, lustful desires, envy, slander, pride and foolishness. All these vile things come from within; they are what defile you.'[32] Jesus' parables are significant for their simplicity and depth. Read again the story of the lost sheep where He pictures Himself as a shepherd and us as sheep:

> So Jesus told them this story: 'If a man has a hundred sheep and one of them gets lost, what will he do? Won't he leave the ninety-nine others in the wilderness and go to search for the one that is lost until he finds it? And when he has found it, he will joyfully carry it home on his shoulders. When he arrives, he will call together his friends and neighbours, saying, "Rejoice with me because I have found my lost sheep." In the same way, there is more joy in heaven over one lost sinner who repents and

returns to God than over ninety-nine others who are righteous and haven't strayed away!'[33]

A little later, Jesus taught the story we call 'The prodigal son', though in Germany they entitle it 'The waiting Father'. It pictures us as wayward but loved, though Jesus also verbally highlighted the smugness of religious hypocrites in His character of the 'older brother'.

A man had two sons. The younger son told his father, 'I want my share of your estate now before you die.' So his father agreed to divide his wealth between his sons. A few days later, this younger son packed all his belongings and moved to a distant land, and there he wasted all his money in wild living. About the time his money ran out, a great famine swept over the land, and he began to starve. He persuaded a local farmer to hire him, and the man sent him into his fields to feed the pigs. The young man became so hungry that even the pods he was feeding the pigs looked good to him. But no one gave him anything.

When he finally came to his senses, he said to himself, 'At home even the hired servants have food enough to spare, and here I am dying of hunger! I will go home to my father and say, "Father, I have sinned against both heaven and you, and I am no longer worthy of being called your son. Please take me on as a hired servant."'

So he returned home to his father. And while he was still a long way off, his father saw him coming. Filled with love and compassion, he ran to his son, embraced him, and kissed him. His son said to him, 'Father, I have sinned against both heaven and you, and I am no longer worthy of being called your son.'

But his father said to the servants, 'Quick! Bring the finest robe in the house and put it on him. Get a ring for his finger and sandals for his feet. And kill the calf we have been fattening. We must celebrate with a feast, for this son of mine was dead and has now returned to life. He was lost, but now he is found.' So the party began.

Meanwhile, the older son was in the fields working. When he returned home, he heard music and dancing in the house, and he asked one of the servants what was going on. 'Your brother is back,' he was told, 'and your father has killed the fattened calf. We are celebrating because of his safe return.'

The older brother was angry and wouldn't go in. His father came out and begged him, but he replied, 'All these years I've slaved for you and never once refused to do a single thing you told me to. And in all that time you never gave me even one young goat for a feast with my friends. Yet when this son of yours comes back after squandering your money on prostitutes, you celebrate by killing the fattened calf!'

His father said to him, 'Look, dear son, you have always stayed by me, and everything I have is yours. We had to celebrate this happy day. For your brother was dead and has come back to life! He was lost, but now he is found!'[34]

In Jesus' story of 'The Good Samaritan', He not only taught to care for the abused, the neglected and the stranger, but He pictured Himself as the One who reaches out to us who have fallen foul of wrongdoing. Again, Jesus is critical of the religious leaders who are bound up in their own busy worlds, but neglect the hurting world around them:

> One day an expert in religious law stood up to test Jesus by asking Him this question, 'Teacher, what should I do to inherit eternal life?'
>
> Jesus replied, 'What does the law of Moses say? How do you read it?'
>
> The man answered, 'You must love the LORD your God with all your heart, all your soul, all your strength, and all your mind; and your neighbour as yourself.'
>
> 'Right!' Jesus told him. 'Do this and you will live!'
>
> The man wanted to justify his actions, so he asked Jesus, 'And who is my neighbour?'
>
> Jesus replied with a story: 'A Jewish man was travelling on a trip from Jerusalem to Jericho, and he was attacked by bandits. They stripped him of his clothes, beat him up, and left him half-dead beside the road.
>
> 'By chance a priest came along. But when he saw the man lying there, he crossed to the other side of the road and passed him by. A Temple assistant walked over and

looked at him lying there, but he also passed by on the other side.

'Then a despised Samaritan came along, and when he saw the man, he felt compassion for him. Going over to him, the Samaritan soothed his wounds with olive oil and wine and bandaged them. Then he put the man on his own donkey and took him to an inn, where he took care of him. The next day he handed the innkeeper two silver coins, telling him, "Take care of this man. If his bill runs higher than this, I'll pay you the next time I'm here."

'Now which of these three would you say was a neighbour to the man who was attacked by bandits?' Jesus asked.

The man replied, 'The one who showed him mercy.'

Then Jesus said, 'Yes, now go and do the same.'[35]

Perhaps it would not have always been comfortable to be near Jesus, as He challenged the preconceptions, the world view, the lives of those around Him, but it was never dull. He was always interesting to be with, to watch, to listen to, to learn from. He oozed sincere authenticity. He discriminated against no one. He was there for the outcasts of society. He would not be silenced by anyone, but neither did He speak for the sake of doing so. When He had something to say, He had to say it. What a man was Jesus, and though many have not wanted Him, He promised that, to as many as received Him, He gave the right to become the children of God.[36]

ENDNOTES

1. Genesis 3:15 and Isaiah 7:14
2. Micah 5:2
3. Psalm 110:1
4. Isaiah 40:3
5. Isaiah 35:5 & 6a
6. Psalm 78:2
7. Psalm 41:9
8. Zechariah 11:12
9. Zechariah 13:7
10. Isaiah 53:7
11. Isaiah 50:6 and Micah 5:1
12. Psalm 22:7 & 8
13. Psalm 22:16 and Zechariah 12:10
14. Isaiah 53:12
15. Isaiah 53:12
16. Isaiah 53:3
17. Psalm 69:4 and Isaiah 49:7
18. Psalm 22:18
19. Psalm 69:21
20. Psalm 34:20
21. Zechariah 12:10
22. Amos 8:9
23. Isaiah 53:9
24. Psalm 16:10; 30:3; 41:10; 118:17 and Hosea 6:2
25. Psalm 68:18a
26. Isaiah 9:6 & 7
27. Such as Cornelius Tacitus, Suetonius and Pliny the Younger.
28. Notably Flavius Josephus.
29. Matthew 13:55 & 56 where we read of Jesus' brothers: James, Joses, Simon and Judas. See also Mark 6:3.
30. Isaiah 9:6-7 (NKJV)
31. John 1:1, 14 (NIV)
32. Mark 7:20-23
33. Luke 15:3-7
34. Luke 15:11-32
35. Luke 10:25-37
36. See John 1:11 and 12

Three

He is the Son of God
... and we should hear Him

The death of Socrates, philosophising quietly with his friends, is the pleasantest that one could desire: that of Jesus, expiring amid torments, insulted, railed at, cursed by a whole nation, is the most horrible that anyone could fear. Socrates, taking the poisoned cup, blesses him who presents it, and weeps beside him. Jesus, in the midst of frightful anguish, prays for his maddened executioners. Yes! If the life and death of Socrates are those of a philosopher, the life and death of Jesus are those of a God.

Jean-Jâcques Rousseau
18th-century philosopher

The Bible makes it clear that there is only one God. Yet in the one God is multiple personality. He is God in three persons: Father, Son and Holy Spirit.[1] There is plurality-in-unity in the Godhead. The Son of God has always been, but in His incarnation – His conception and birth – He took on Himself human flesh. God took upon Himself humanity.

Jesus began His preaching and teaching at the age of thirty, working in the towns and villages around the Sea of Galilee. In the Old Testament, Moses, speaking to God, asked Him by what name He should be called. God answered by saying that He was to be called 'I am'.

It is significant that it was this name that Jesus took on Himself. He said:

> *I am* the Way, the Truth and the Life; no one comes to the Father but by Me.

> *I am* the true vine

> *I am* the door

> *I am* the Good Shepherd

> *I am* the Resurrection and the Life

Each time Jesus used that term, He was saying in His language, 'I am God Himself.' His listeners understood exactly what He was saying, so that when Jesus said,

> 'Before Abraham was, *I am.*'

the people took up stones to throw at Him. Some of them hated the fact that Jesus was saying that He was God, yet He was simply introducing Himself to them.

On three occasions we read in the Bible that God spoke from heaven affirming that Jesus is God. On two of those occasions He simply said, 'This is my beloved Son, hear Him.'[2]

Jesus is as much a man as any man is man; but He is as much God as God is God. Jesus did not lay aside His deity when He took on Himself human form. He called people to leave everything and follow Him, an act which would be audacious and brash if He were not God. He

accepted worship, as only God would. He commended
Mary for simply soaking up all that He had to say:

> As Jesus and the disciples continued on their way to
> Jerusalem, they came to a certain village where a woman
> named Martha welcomed Him into her home. Her
> sister, Mary, sat at the Lord's feet, listening to what He
> taught. But Martha was distracted by the big dinner she
> was preparing. She came to Jesus and said, 'Lord, doesn't
> it seem unfair to you that my sister just sits here while
> I do all the work? Tell her to come and help me.'
>
> But the Lord said to her, 'My dear Martha, you are
> worried and upset over all these details! There is only
> one thing worth being concerned about. Mary has
> discovered it, and it will not be taken away from her.'[3]

Jesus believed the Old Testament, the part of the Bible
written before His birth, as the Word of God. That is
hardly surprising as so much of the Old Testament is
a straight record of what God said, so that phrases such
as 'Thus says the Lord …' are commonplace. But what
is staggering, except that He is Himself God, is that
He said that the Old Testament was speaking about
Himself![4] Jesus is the theme of the Bible: it prophesies
Him, pictures and portrays Him, and anticipates Him,
then after His birth it describes Him, explains His work,
applies His achievements and anticipates His kingly rule
while all the time honouring Him, and thrilling us with
His person.

Recalling some of the things that Jesus did, it is evident that they were things that only God could do. Jesus gave sight to the blind, hearing to the deaf, speech to the mute, healing to lepers, strength to the paralysed. He cast out demons from people who were possessed by the power of Satan. He raised the dead, bringing back to life young and old.

He brought immediate calm to the storm and sea, so that even the wind and the waves obeyed Him. On one occasion He took just five loaves and two fish, and fed over 5,000 people, and on another occasion seven loaves and a few fish, and fed over 4,000 people who had been listening to Him.[5] The feeding of the 5,000 is found in each of the four Gospels. Reading the passage underlines the calm yet authoritative way that Jesus took control of the situation and brought about a resolution to the issue of hungry crowds that was in keeping with who He really was.

Jesus turned water into wine; He walked on water. Only the Creator of all things possesses these powers.

Even more striking is that Jesus forgave sin. Only God can do that because sin is primarily an offence toward God. In this first example, it is clear that Jesus and His enemies knew exactly what He was doing and saying when He forgave a man whose sin was so serious it led to physical illness:

Jesus climbed into a boat and went back across the lake to His own town. Some people brought to Him a paralysed man on a mat. Seeing their faith, Jesus said to the paralysed man, 'Be encouraged, my child! Your sins are forgiven.' But some of the teachers of religious law said to themselves, 'That's blasphemy! Does he think he's God?'

Jesus knew what they were thinking, so He asked them, 'Why do you have such evil thoughts in your hearts? Is it easier to say, "Your sins are forgiven," or "Stand up and walk"? So I will prove to you that the Son of Man has the authority on earth to forgive sins.' Then Jesus turned to the paralysed man and said, 'Stand up, pick up your mat, and go home!'

And the man jumped up and went home! Fear swept through the crowd as they saw this happen. And they praised God for sending a man with such great authority.[6]

On another occasion, a woman was dragged before Jesus accused of committing adultery. The religious leaders wanted her stoned to death. Strangely, they had left alone the man with whom she was involved. Some have suggested that maybe he was one of their number, but we don't know. As far as the teachers of the religious law and the Pharisees were concerned, the woman had no soul, no personality; she was just a pawn to be used in building their case against Jesus. He in turn cleverly pointed out that they too were sinners. When He challenged them, saying that the one who was sinless among them should throw the first stone at her, they were disturbed. Only Jesus was qualified, but He did not want to stone her!

Jesus returned to the Mount of Olives, but early the next morning He was back again at the Temple. A crowd soon gathered, and He sat down and taught them. As He was speaking, the teachers of religious law and the Pharisees brought a woman who had been caught in the act of adultery. They put her in front of the crowd.

'Teacher,' they said to Jesus, 'this woman was caught in the act of adultery. The law of Moses says to stone her. What do you say?'

They were trying to trap Him into saying something they could use against Him, but Jesus stooped down and wrote in the dust with His finger. They kept demanding an answer, so He stood up again and said, 'All right, but let the one who has never sinned throw the first stone!' Then He stooped down again and wrote in the dust.

When the accusers heard this, they slipped away one by one, beginning with the oldest, until only Jesus was left in the middle of the crowd with the woman. Then Jesus stood up again and said to the woman, 'Where are your accusers? Didn't even one of them condemn you?'

'No, Lord' she said.

And Jesus said, 'Neither do I. Go and sin no more.'

Jesus spoke to the people once more and said, 'I am the light of the world. If you follow me, you won't have to walk in darkness, because you will have the light that leads to life.'[7]

The final sentence is important. Jesus turned back to the crowd to whom He had been speaking and drew the whole incident to a conclusion, teaching that when gospel light shines it reveals sin. When sin is shown up, you can either walk away from Jesus and remain in your sin, as did the religious leaders, or stay with Him and let Him deal with it, which is what the woman did. However, He could say that He didn't condemn the woman because of who He was, namely the Lord, the Judge of all.

Reading the Gospels and seeing what Jesus said not only about forgiveness, but on every subject, it becomes clear that His words are not those of merely a great orator who could work the crowds, but original, authoritative and godly. His Sermon on the Mount began with what we call the Beatitudes. They are profound. It is God speaking words which run against the grain of today's secular society:

Now when He saw the crowds, He went up on a mountainside and sat down. His disciples came to Him, and He began to teach them saying:

' Blessed are the poor in spirit,
     for theirs is the kingdom of heaven.
' Blessed are those who mourn,
     for they will be comforted.
' Blessed are the meek,
     for they will inherit the earth.

'Blessed are those who hunger and thirst for righteousness,
      for they will be filled.
'Blessed are the merciful,
      for they will be shown mercy.
'Blessed are the pure in heart,
      for they will see God.
'Blessed are the peacemakers,
      for they will be called sons of God.
'Blessed are those who are persecuted because of righteousness,
      for theirs is the kingdom of heaven.
'Blessed are you when people insult you, persecute you
and falsely say all kinds of evil against you because of
me. Rejoice and be glad, because great is your reward in
heaven, for in the same way they persecuted the prophets
who were before you.'[8]

C. S. Lewis, professor of Medieval and Renaissance
literature at Cambridge University, wrote in his famous
book, *Mere Christianity*: 'Jesus … told people that their
sins were forgiven … This makes sense only if He really
was the God whose laws are broken and whose love is
wounded in every sin.' And to quote him again:

I am trying here to prevent anyone saying the really
foolish thing that people often say about Him:'I'm ready
to accept Jesus as a great moral teacher, but I don't accept
His claim to be God.' That is the one thing we must not
say. A man who was merely a man and said the sort of
things Jesus said would not be a great moral teacher.

He would either be a lunatic – on a level with the man who says he is a poached egg – or else he would be the Devil of Hell. You must make your choice. Either this man was, and is, the Son of God: or else a madman or something worse. You can shut Him up for a fool, you can spit at Him and kill Him as a demon; or you can fall at His feet and call Him Lord and God. But let us not come with any patronising nonsense about His being a great moral teacher. He has not left that open to us. He did not intend to.

Jesus lived a perfect life. He was without sin. When He asked which person could convince Him of committing any sin, there was total silence. Even His enemies testified to His purity: Judas, who sold Jesus for thirty pieces of silver, committed suicide with the words, 'I have betrayed innocent blood'; Pontius Pilate, the governor who legally tried Jesus, appealed to the crowd who were baying for Jesus' blood, asking them, 'Why, what evil has He done? I find no fault in Him.' The Roman soldier who was responsible for the execution of Jesus said, 'Surely, this Man was the Son of God!' Those who were closest to Him testified in the same way. John, the disciple who was closest to Jesus, said of Him, '*In Him* was no sin'; Peter, the disciple full of action, wrote, 'He did no sin'; Paul, the great intellectual, said, 'He *knew* no sin'; and the Book of Hebrews comments, 'He was *without* sin'. Even Jesus' mother, Mary, literally worshipped Jesus.

When Jesus hung on the cross, carrying the sin of the world on Himself, He again was showing that He was God. Such love only comes from God. But to carry the weight of the world's sin on Himself and pay for it in three hours, He had to be God. If He were only human, that sin would have destroyed His mind – He would not have been able to bear the emotional strain – but as God He paid for all sin, so that we could be forgiven.

Only God has power to conquer death. Jesus, who died, was buried. Three days later, He rose again. In every work of God throughout the Bible, the Father, the Son and the Holy Spirit were at work. Each person of the Holy Trinity was involved in creating the world, in the incarnation of Jesus (His becoming a man and making earth His home), in the baptism of Jesus, His death and His resurrection. We read that the Father raised Jesus back to life, that the Holy Spirit did so, and that Jesus raised Himself from the dead.[9] The four Gospel writers reveal different details of the resurrection of Jesus, and they are all wonderful to read, but Matthew describes it this way:

> Early on Sunday morning, as the new day was dawning, Mary Magdalene and the other Mary went out to visit the tomb.
>
> Suddenly there was a great earthquake! For an angel of the Lord came down from heaven, rolled aside the stone, and sat on it. His face shone like lightning, and his

clothing was as white as snow. The guards shook with fear when they saw him, and they fell into a dead faint.

Then the angel spoke to the women. 'Don't be afraid!' he said. 'I know you are looking for Jesus, who was crucified. He isn't here! He is risen from the dead, just as He said would happen. Come, see where His body was lying. And now, go quickly and tell His disciples that He has risen from the dead, and He is going ahead of you to Galilee. You will see Him there. Remember what I have told you.'

The women ran quickly from the tomb. They were very frightened but also filled with great joy, and they rushed to give the disciples the angel's message. And as they went, Jesus met them and greeted them. And they ran to Him, grasped His feet, and worshipped Him.[10]

Samantha Roberts is the articulate Yorkshire widow of the first serviceman to be killed in the second Iraq war. She longed for an apology from the Defence Secretary, Geoff Hoon, because her husband was never given proper defensive clothing, but that apology never came. However, when the President of the U.S.A. visited England she was presented to him. They chatted for a little while, and the media were keen to know what they had said. She simply told them, 'I have just met the most powerful man in the world, but he couldn't bring back my husband!'

The resurrection of Jesus is absolutely central to the gospel message. As the historian Arnold Toynbee said in his book *Man's Concern with Death*, 'Find the body of that Jew, and Christianity crumbles into ruins.' Of course, that will never happen because He is risen and ascended to heaven.

When Jesus rose again from the dead, He showed Himself risen to Mary and Mary Magdalene, to Peter and John, to ten of the disciples, and then to doubting Thomas who was absent earlier. He showed Himself to two people walking the seven miles from Jerusalem to Emmaus, and then later to the apostle Paul. Unlike all other political or religious leaders of the past, Jesus has no grave or tombstone. He left behind Him grave clothes and an empty tomb.

In the four accounts of the life of the Lord Jesus in the Bible – Matthew, Mark, Luke and John – the Gospel of Matthew looks at Jesus as the King who fulfilled all the Old Testament prophecies about the Messiah; Mark's Gospel focuses on Jesus the servant, in a hurry to meet the needs of men and women; the Gospel of Luke looks at Jesus as the Son of Man who has come to save those who are lost; and John's Gospel is about Jesus the Son of God in whom, if we believe, we will have eternal life.

One day Jesus will return again, not this time as a babe in a manger, but as the Lord, the King, and He will reign over all. The Bible says that one day every knee will bow and acknowledge Him as Lord over all. Imagine: all atheists, tyrants, terrorists, paedophiles, lager louts, celebrities applauded by society, adherents of every religion, as well as the self-righteous who felt they never needed Jesus, or those who simply kept God at a distance, plus you and I, will confess Jesus as Lord. Jesus of Nazareth, born in Bethlehem, crucified at Calvary, now raised from the dead, will rule over all. He will take His rightful position as the Son of God.

Someone has worked out that about eight per cent of the New Testament is devoted to this great theme of Jesus returning to judge the earth. For Christians, it is something wonderful to look forward to, but for those who have rejected Him, it will be an awful time of regret and remorse. Look at just a little of what Jesus Himself taught on this subject:

> As Jesus was leaving the Temple grounds, His disciples pointed out to Him the various Temple buildings. But He responded, 'Do you see all these buildings? I tell you the truth, they will be completely demolished. Not one stone will be left on top of another!'
>
> Later, Jesus sat on the Mount of Olives. His disciples came to Him privately and said, 'Tell us, when will all this happen? What sign will signal your return and the end of the world?'
>
> Jesus told them, 'Don't let anyone mislead you, for many will come in my name, claiming, "I am the Messiah". They will deceive many. And you will hear of wars and threats of wars, but don't panic. Yes, these things must take place, but the end won't follow immediately. Nation will go to war against nation, and kingdom against

kingdom. There will be famines and earthquakes in many parts of the world. But all this is only the first of the birth pains, with more to come.

'Then you will be arrested, persecuted, and killed. You will be hated all over the world because you are my followers. And many will turn away from me and betray and hate each other. And many false prophets will appear and will deceive many people. Sin will be rampant everywhere, and the love of many will grow cold. But the one who endures to the end will be saved. And the Good News about the Kingdom will be preached throughout the whole world, so that all nations will hear it; and then the end will come....

'Immediately after the anguish of those days,

> the sun will be darkened,
> the moon will give no light,
> the stars will fall from the sky,
> and the powers in the heavens will be shaken.

'And then at last, the sign that the Son of Man is coming will appear in the heavens, and there will be deep mourning among all the peoples of the earth. And they will see the Son of Man coming on the clouds of heaven with power and great glory. And He will send out His angels with the mighty blast of a trumpet, and they will gather His chosen ones from all over the world – from the farthest ends of the earth and heaven.'

' …no one knows the day or hour when these things will happen, not even the angels in heaven or the Son himself. Only the Father knows.

'When the Son of Man returns, it will be like it was in Noah's day. In those days before the flood, the people were enjoying banquets and parties and weddings right up to the time Noah entered his boat. People didn't realize what was going to happen until the flood came and swept them all away. That is the way it will be when the Son of Man comes.

'Two men will be working together in the field; one will be taken, the other left. Two women will be grinding flour at the mill; one will be taken, the other left.

'So you, too, must keep watch! For you don't know what day your Lord is coming. Understand this: If a homeowner knew exactly when a burglar was coming, he would keep watch and not permit his house to be broken into. You also must be ready all the time, for the Son of Man will come when least expected.'[11]

Either Jesus was completely obsessed with Himself as a megalomaniac who needed psychiatric care, or He was deceiving us, or He was and is the Lord of Heaven who walked on earth and will one day be the acknowledged Lord of all. When God spoke about His Son, He said, 'Hear Him', which is still the wisest of things to do.

ENDNOTES

1. Interestingly, the Bible teaches that God made Adam in His own image. And we, as human beings, are like God in that we are individuals, but comprising body, soul and spirit. See 1 Thessalonians 5:23.
2. Matthew 3:17, 17:5 and John 12:28.
3. Luke 10:38-42
4. See Luke 24:13-32.
5. Matthew 14:15-21, 15:32-38, and 16:8-10
6. Matthew 9:1-8
7. John 8:1-12
8. Matthew 5:1-12 (NIV)
9. John 2:19-22; Acts 5:30; Romans 1:4.
10. Matthew 28:1-9
11. Extracts taken from Matthew 24

FOUR

He is the Lamb of God
... and we should look to Him

As Man alone, Jesus could not have saved us; as God alone, He would not; Incarnate, He could and did.

Malcolm Muggeridge
journalist and broadcaster

Of the literally hundreds of names given to the Lord Jesus in the Bible, one of the more intriguing ones is 'Lamb of God'. Of course, the word 'lamb' kindles the thought of innocence and newness. Jesus was without sin, and was crucified at the age of just thirty-three, but there is more signified in this phrase 'Lamb of God'.

John the Baptist, the cousin of Jesus, was born six months before Him. He was quite a character, attracting large crowds to hear his powerful, forthright preaching. Eventually, after speaking against the adultery of King Herod, he was imprisoned and later beheaded. Once when he was preaching he saw Jesus coming towards him. John stopped the flow of his message, pointed everyone's attention to Jesus with the words, 'Look! The Lamb of God who takes away the sin of the world!'[1] The same thing happened the next day as John was with two of his disciples.

Jewish listeners would have understood what John was saying. They knew that if they felt conscious of their own wrongdoing, God had given instruction that they had to take a substitute animal to the Jewish priest in the temple and, as they laid their hand on the animal, it would die and they would walk away forgiven. The lamb was known to be the innocent sacrifice, which died in place of the guilty person. It died, taking on itself the penalty of sin, so that the sinner could walk away forgiven and free. John had understood that Jesus was to die, the guiltless instead of the guilty, so that we might be set free and be forgiven.

This is the great truth that is at the very heart of the Christian message. In fact, as you read much of the New Testament, it is almost as if Jesus came to do just three days' work, because His death and resurrection are the events which are so crucial to the gospel story. Jesus came into the world primarily with the purpose of laying down His life as a substitute sacrifice for our sin. Jesus came not so much to proclaim the gospel but that there might be a gospel to proclaim. Sin is the breaking of God's commandments. It is failing to love God and to love others as we ought. It brings judgment as it cuts us off from God, keeps us out of heaven and would condemn us to hell. Jesus died, carrying on Himself the sins of the ages and of all individuals. The Bible says that He was made sin for us. He died, the Righteous One, in place of us, the unrighteous ones, that He might bring us to God. In hours of time on the cross, Jesus became the greatest liar, thief, adulterer, blasphemer and murderer that humanity has ever known – not because He committed any of these sins, but because He was actually made sin for us.

Crucifixion is one of the worst forms of capital punishment ever devised in the history of humanity. It was first practised by the Phoenicians 300 years before Christ. In the world today where there is capital punishment it is usually quick and private. Crucifixion was slow and public. It was intended to be a deterrent. Long before crucifixions began, and longer before Jesus was born, the Old Testament prophets had said that when the Christ came He would be crucified, and He would die carrying the sin of the world on His shoulders. This is how Mark describes the crucifixion of Jesus:

> The soldiers took Jesus into the courtyard of the governor's headquarters (called the Praetorium) and called out the entire regiment. They dressed Him in a purple robe, and they wove thorn branches into a crown and put it on His head. Then they saluted Him and taunted, 'Hail! King of the Jews!' And they struck Him on the head with a reed

stick, spit on Him and dropped to their knees in mock worship. When they were finally tired of mocking Him, they took off the purple robe and put His own clothes on Him again. Then they led Him away to be crucified.

A passer-by named Simon, who was from Cyrene, was coming in from the countryside just then, and the soldiers forced him to carry Jesus' cross. (Simon was the father of Alexander and Rufus.) And they brought Jesus to a place called Golgotha (which means Place of the Skull). They offered Him wine drugged with myrrh, but He refused it.

Then the soldiers nailed Him to the cross. They divided His clothes and threw dice to decide who would get each piece. It was nine o'clock in the morning when they crucified Him. A sign was fastened to the cross, announcing the charge against Him. It read: 'The King of the Jews'. Two revolutionaries were crucified with Him, one on His right and one on His left.

The people passing by shouted abuse, shaking their heads in mockery. 'Ha! Look at you now!' they yelled at Him. 'You said you were going to destroy the Temple and rebuild it in three days. Well then, save yourself and come down from the cross!'

The leading priests and teachers of religious law also mocked Jesus. 'He saved others,' they scoffed, 'but he can't save himself! Let this Messiah, this King of Israel, come down from the cross so we can see it and believe Him!' Even the men who were crucified with Jesus ridiculed Him.

At noon, darkness fell across the whole land until three o'clock. Then at three o'clock Jesus called out with a loud voice, 'Eloi, Eloi, lama sabachthani?' which means 'My God, my God, why have you abandoned me?'

Some of the bystanders misunderstood and thought He was calling for the prophet Elijah. One of them ran and filled a sponge with sour wine, holding it up to Him on a reed stick so He could drink. 'Wait!' he said. 'Let's see whether Elijah comes to take Him down!'

Then Jesus uttered another loud cry and breathed His last. And the curtain in the sanctuary of the Temple was torn in two, from top to bottom.

When the Roman officer who stood facing Him saw how He had died, he exclaimed, 'This man truly was the Son of God!'

Some women were there, watching from a distance, including Mary Magdalene, Mary (the mother of James the younger and of Joseph), and Salome. They had been followers of Jesus and had cared for Him while He was in Galilee. Many other women who had come with Him to Jerusalem were also there.[2]

(For a detailed description of crucifixion, please see the Note on Crucifixion p. 57 at the end of this chapter.)

Jesus was not killed, though it was the intention of His executioners to murder Him. He had previously said, 'No one can take my life; I have power to lay it down and I have power to take it up again.' He said, 'I am the way, the truth and the life …' and 'I am the resurrection and the life.' No one could take away His life. But on the cross, when He had fully paid the price of sin, He said in a loud voice, 'It is finished', then praying, said, 'Father, into your hands I commit my spirit' as He dismissed His spirit and gave up His life. He is the only one in history who chose to die. Even those who commit suicide only choose how, where and when they will die. They would eventually have died if they hadn't shortened their lives. Jesus need never have died, but out of love gave up His life for us. As Augustine wrote nearly 1,700 years ago, 'I can see the depths of God, but I cannot see the bottom.'

Mel Gibson's film *The Passion of the Christ* graphically portrays the physical and even the emotional suffering of Jesus. What no actor can ever portray is what Jesus suffered spiritually. He who was absolutely pure, took on Himself the filth, the sin of the world. Jesus was at one with His Father throughout eternity, but in the three hours of darkness, Jesus was mysteriously cut off from Him. As He entered into His suffering on the cross and as He came out of those hours, He prayed to His Father. But as He carried our sins, He could only pray to 'God' saying, 'My God, my God, why have You forsaken Me?' Jesus was forsaken by God so that we might be forgiven and never be forsaken by God.

I remember the story of a cynical Chicago-based journalist who was sent to cover a series of huge gospel meetings at which the American evangelist, Billy Graham, was preaching. He had every intention of writing derisively about what he was about to witness. Tens of thousands of

Jesus, the Lamb of God

people gathered, which bewildered the journalist. Before
Billy Graham preached, an elderly gospel singer, George
Beverly Shea, sang a solo, the lyrics of which were penned
by John Newton 250 years earlier (he had also written the
song 'Amazing Grace'). The words were:

> I saw One hanging on a tree,
> In agony and blood,
> Who fixed His languid eyes on me,
> As near His cross I stood.
>
> O, can it be, upon a tree,
> The Saviour died for me?
> My soul is thrilled, my heart is filled,
> To think He died for me!
>
> Sure, never to my latest breath,
> Can I forget that look;
> It seemed to charge me with His death,
> Though not a word He spoke.
>
> My conscience felt and owned the guilt,
> And plunged me in despair,
> I saw my sins His blood had spilt,
> And helped to nail Him there.
>
> A second look He gave, which said,
> 'I freely all forgive;
> This blood is for thy ransom paid;
> I die that thou may'st live.'

Before the song was completed, the pencil dropped from the journalist's lips and repeatedly he muttered, 'Just to think, He died for me … just to think, He died for me …' Before the sermon had even begun, the reporter had been converted to Christ. He had trusted Jesus as his Lord and Saviour. It was that Jesus had loved him enough to die for him that convinced him.

The apostle Peter, writing as an old man to Christians scattered throughout the world, said:

> Christ suffered for you. He is your example, and you must follow in His steps.
>
> He never sinned, nor ever deceived anyone. He did not retaliate when He was insulted, nor threaten revenge when He suffered. He left His case in the hands of God, who always judges fairly. He personally carried our sins in His body on the cross so that we can be dead to sin and live for what is right. By His wounds you are healed. Once you were like sheep who wandered away. But now you have turned to your Shepherd, the Guardian of your souls.[3]

In the Bible God says, 'Look unto Me, all you ends of the earth, and be saved.' God wants us to 'look' to Jesus crucified and risen, and to take Him as our own. However, the moment we trust Jesus as Lord and Saviour, not only do we find that He carried our sins on the cross 2,000 years ago, but He immediately transfers to us His goodness. Our sins have been laid on Jesus, now His righteousness clothes us. It is a two-way transfer. And it happens when a person is converted, when they put their trust in Jesus.

Five hundred years ago the German reformer, Martin Luther, discovered the same truth. It was the catalyst of a change which was to impact all of Europe. Born in Eisleben in 1483, the son of a coal miner, Luther was first a lawyer, and then became a monk and professor of biblical studies at Wittenberg University. But he struggled with his conscience which seemed to accuse him of so much sin. He did everything he could to try to remove his guilt. Eventually, he travelled from Germany to Rome in his search for forgiveness and God. As he crawled up the Scala Santa steps in Rome, he kissed each one and prayed to 'the Virgin Mary'. But upon completion he still knew his sins were not forgiven.

Filling his mind, though, were the Bible words, 'The just shall live by faith'. For years he had worked to try to buy forgiveness but without success. Now it was dawning on him that Jesus had paid for his sins, and that heaven was not a reward but a gift. He came to a clear understanding that salvation was through faith in Jesus alone, when he was in his early thirties. Trusting Jesus alone, Luther found forgiveness, new life and a passion to tell everyone that only Jesus can take away sin.

Whether an American journalist, or a German reformer, the important issue is the need to recognize who Jesus is, what He has done, and then to 'look' to Him. Looking to Jesus means that we cease to rely on anything in ourselves to earn us favour with God, but to trust Jesus alone to forgive us, and bring us to know God as Father, as a Friend forever.

ENDNOTES

1. John 1:29
2. Mark 15:16-41.
3. 1 Peter 2:21-25

CRUCIFIXION

What is crucifixion? A medical doctor provides a physical description.

The cross is placed on the ground and the exhausted man is quickly thrown backwards with his shoulders against the wood. The legionnaire feels for the depression at the front of the wrist. He drives a heavy, square, wrought-iron nail through the wrist and deep into the wood. Quickly he moves to the other side and repeats the action, being careful not to pull the arms too tightly, but to allow some flex and movement. The cross is then lifted into place. The left foot is pressed backward against the right foot, and with both feet extended, toes down, a nail is driven through the arch of each, leaving the knees flexed. The victim is now crucified. As he slowly sags down with more weight on the nails in the wrists, excruciating, fiery pain shoots along the fingers and up the arms to explode in the brain – the nails in the wrists are putting pressure on the median nerves. As he pushes himself upward to avoid this stretching torment, he places the full weight on the nail through his feet. Again he feels the searing agony of the nail tearing through the nerves between the bones of his feet.

As the arms fatigue, cramps sweep through the muscles, knotting them in deep, relentless, throbbing pain. With these cramps comes the inability to push himself upward to breathe. Air can be drawn into the lungs but not exhaled. He fights to raise himself in order to get even one small breath. Finally, carbon dioxide builds up in the lungs and in the bloodstream, and the cramps partially subside. Spasmodically he is able to push himself upward to exhale and bring in life-giving oxygen. He suffers hours of this limitless pain, cycles of twisting, joint-rending cramps, intermittent partial asphyxiation, searing pain as tissue is torn from his lacerated back as he moves up and down against the rough timber. Then another agony begins: a deep, crushing pain deep in the chest as the pericardium slowly fills with serum and begins to compress the heart. It is now almost over – the loss of tissue fluids has reached a critical level – the compressed heart is struggling to pump heavy, thick, sluggish blood into the tissues, the tortured lungs are making a frantic effort to gasp in small gulps of air. He can feel the chill of death creeping through his tissues. Finally, he can allow his body to die.

(Adapted from C. Truman Davis M.D. in *The Expositor's Bible Commentary*, vol. 8)

Five

He is the Way to God
... and we should come to Him

In the evening I went very unwilling to a society in Aldersgate Street, where someone was reading (Martin) Luther's preface to the epistle to the Romans. About a quarter before nine, while he was describing the change which God works in the heart through faith in Christ, I felt my heart strangely warmed. I felt I did trust in Christ, Christ alone for salvation; and an assurance was given me that He had taken away my sins, even mine, and saved me from the law of sin and death.

John Wesley
preacher and evangelist, (describing
his conversion on 24th May, 1738)

I know it is only a children's story but C. S. Lewis has a memorable passage in his book *The Silver Chair*, written in 1953, which illustrates the fact that we all have deep spiritual needs. Jesus is more than a figure of history; He is Lord, He is the Saviour, and without Him we are lost. He only can satisfy our deepest needs and bring us into a living relationship with God that lasts for eternity. For the context, do read C. S. Lewis's book, but for the moment this quotation will suffice:

'Are you thirsty?' said the Lion.
'I'm DYING of thirst,' said Jill.

'Then drink,' said the Lion.

'May I – could I – would you mind going away while I do?' said Jill.

The Lion answered this only by a look and a very low growl. And as Jill gazed at its motionless bulk, she realized that she might as well have asked the whole mountain to move aside for her convenience. The delicious rippling noise of the stream was driving her nearly frantic.

'Will you promise not to do anything to me, if I come?' said Jill.

'I make no promise,' said the Lion.

Jill was so thirsty now that, without noticing it, she had come a step nearer. 'Do you eat girls?' she said.

'I have swallowed up girls and boys, women and men, kings and emperors, cities and realms,' said the Lion. It didn't say this as if it were boasting, nor as if it were sorry, nor as if it were angry. It just said it.

'I daren't come and drink,' said Jill.

'Then you will die of thirst,' said the Lion.

'O dear!' said Jill, coming another step nearer. 'I suppose I must go and look for another stream then.'

'There is no other stream,' said the Lion.

For so many there is a deep-seated sense of emptiness. Ex-Cabinet minister and now a widely respected compère on Classic FM, David Mellor, was quoted recently as saying, 'Everything I have done in life has been redundant. My life has been one long exercise in futility.'[1] BBC Radio 5 Live anchorman, Richard Bacon, said more or less the same to someone who phoned in to his programme: 'I don't mind superficiality – that's the currency of my life.'[2] Such expressions are inevitable if life is lived without God. Jesus frequently had people ask Him about 'life', no doubt because they recognized that He knew what real life was. He repeatedly said that He was 'the life' and then made it clear that He had come 'that they may have life and have it more abundantly.'[3]

This life is one that is lived in fellowship with God Himself. This life involves knowing that all sin has been forgiven. It includes the dimension of wanting to live in a way that pleases God. It has the promise that it does not exist for time alone, but for all eternity. It gives meaning, purpose and joy, even though at times it is hard and means swimming against the prevailing tides of secularism, materialism and hedonism. Jesus is willing to take us by the hand and lead us through life, then death, and into eternity. No one in the Bible spoke more about heaven and hell than Jesus. He did so tenderly and lovingly, but nevertheless honestly, refusing to avoid unpalatable truths. He who loved us enough to die for us also loved us enough to warn us of the need to be right with God before we meet Him in judgment.

The religions of the world teach that people should work to earn favour with their gods. But the Bible teaches that it is not by our works of righteousness that we can ever reach up to the true and living God. He has come to us. In Jesus, God was on the greatest of all rescue missions. He was reaching out to us, to bring us to God. Jesus said, 'I am the way, the truth and the life. No one comes to the Father but by me.'[4] Peter, one of Jesus' disciples, said, 'There is no other name under heaven, given among men whereby we must be saved',[5] and Paul added, 'There is one God, and one mediator between God and men, the man Christ Jesus.'[6]

Jesus came from God to reach out to men and women, and bring them/us to God. Throughout the Bible God is appealing to men and women to come to Him. In fact, the Bible ends with that very invitation. Jesus told a parable on this theme:

'A man prepared a great feast and sent out many invitations. When the banquet was ready, he sent his servant to tell the guests, "Come, the banquet is ready." But they all began making excuses. One said, "I have just bought a field and must inspect it. Please excuse me." Another said, "I have just bought five pairs of oxen, and I want to try them out. Please excuse me." Another said, "I now have a wife, so I can't come."

'The servant returned and told his master what they had said. His master was furious and said, "Go quickly into the streets and alleys of the town and invite the poor, the crippled, the blind, and the lame." After the servant had done this, he reported, "There is still room for more." So his master said, "Go out into the country lanes and behind the hedges and urge anyone you find to come, so that the house will be full. For none of those I first invited will get even the smallest taste of my banquet." '[7]

The first group of people who were invited one would have expected to have gone to the feast, but instead they made up pathetic excuses that really cut no ice. There were two other types of people: the first needed some persuasion that they really were invited, the second needed compelling, but the fact was that they were all invited to be guests at a great banquet, which was Jesus' picture language to describe the joy of being a follower of His.

Jesus invites us today – in fact He commands us, – to turn from all that is wrong in our lives and find forgiveness and new life in Him. Martin Luther, writing nearly 500 years ago, expressed the significance of our response to Jesus' death and His invitation to us: 'Either sin is with you, lying on your shoulders, or it is lying on Christ, the Lamb of God. Now if it is lying on your back, you are lost; but if it is resting on Christ, you are free, and you will be saved. Now choose what you want.'

When someone loved us so much that He died for us, and when that someone is the Lord God Almighty who came to earth for us, the only rational response is to receive Him in the way He wants.

Throughout the ages when men and women have put their trust in Jesus, He has brought them to a living relationship with Himself that is more real than anything else they have experienced.

A. N. Wilson is one Britain's literary giants. He is a newspaper columnist and author of numerous books, including biographies of Leo Tolstoy, C. S. Lewis, Jesus Christ, as well as the Victorians. Writing in the *New Statesman* and then the *Daily Mail* on Easter Saturday 2009, he described his journey from atheism to belief again, and in a typically journalistic way criticized the smug, self-satisfied unbelief of people like Jonathan Ross, Jo Brand and Polly Toynbee. He wrote:

Like most educated people in Britain and Northern Europe (I was born in 1950), I have grown up in a culture that is overwhelmingly secular and anti-religious. The universities, broadcasters and media generally are not merely non-religious, they are positively anti. To my shame, I believe it was this that made me lose faith and heart in my youth. It felt so uncool to be religious ... for ten or fifteen of my middle years, I too was one of the mockers. But as time passed, I found myself going back to church ... my belief has come about in large measure because of the lives and examples of people I have known – not the famous, not saints, but friends and relations who have lived, and faced death in the light of the Resurrection story, or in the quiet acceptance that they have a future after they die ... Most of the greatest writers and thinkers of the past 1,500 years have believed it. But an even stronger argument is the way that Christian faith transforms individual lives – the lives of men and women with whom you mingle on a daily basis, the man, woman or child next to you in church tomorrow morning.

General Sir Richard Dannatt, Commander of the United Kingdom Land Forces from 2005 to 2009, writes from a very different perspective about the same experience of coming to know Jesus:

> 11th November is the date in the calendar each year when we remember Armistice Day – for it was the 11th hour of the 11th day of the 11th month in 1918 that the surrender of Germany to end the First World War was announced. Surrender is two things – it is the end of the fighting and the beginning of peace. I discovered that 11th November 1977 was the moment that I stopped fighting with God … and that it was the moment that I fully committed myself to Him … I found on that date, that a far better way of life was to commit myself wholeheartedly to Him, to enjoy peace and purpose in life that only full commitment to Jesus Christ can bring.

Dan Walker presents *Football Focus* each Saturday on BBC. He has hit the headlines because of his unwillingness to work on Sundays. For him, though, the defining issue in his life is Jesus. He has always loved football, but everything changed for him one day in 1989 when at church he heard someone preach 'on the importance of knowing Jesus Christ as your personal Saviour'. He says:

[I] was rooted to the spot. For the first time in my life, my mind wasn't wandering ... I felt the depth of my sin. I knew that I was offending God by the life I was living, and the prospect of going to hell terrified me. I wanted to go to heaven – I wanted to be in the presence of God thanks to the saving love of His Son, the Lord Jesus Christ ... that night, I went to bed a different person. I knew that my sins had been forgiven.

By the time Helen Shapiro had turned fifteen, two of her recordings had reached number one in the UK pop charts, the second of them, 'Walking Back to Happiness'.[8] Trumpeter Humphrey Lyttelton described her as one of the great jazz singers of her age. By the age of nineteen, with millions of record sales to her name, she faced huge personal struggles that dogged her for years. Brought up in the Jewish faith, she nevertheless turned to anything for help: hypnotherapists, dozens of doctors, Buddhism, mediums, fortune-telling and a faith healer, but nobody seemed to have the answers she needed. Something was missing but she couldn't discover what it was. She had found *Songs of Praise* on television a dirge, but a fellow musician had impressed her by his life and trust in Jesus. For her, though, the issue was whether Jesus was really the Messiah Jewish people were still awaiting. Careful study led her to the many Old Testament prophecies concerning Jesus, and she saw how perfectly they predicted and portrayed Jesus. She read the four Gospels. About ten-thirty one night in August, when she was forty years of age, she asked 'Yeshua' (Jesus) to forgive her sins and come into her life. She came to the conclusion that it was the most Jewish thing that she had ever done. Jesus had not come to destroy the Old Testament law but fulfil or complete it. She now revels in having a personal relationship with God. She has returned to the God of Abraham, Isaac and Jacob. She now meets with others, Christian believers and those who see themselves not as ex-Jews, but Jews who have come to a fulfilment in Jesus.

Christians not only believe in and trust the Lord Jesus, but they love Him. Here is the testimony of the great Russian novelist Fyodor Dostoevsky: 'I believe there is nothing lovelier, deeper, more sympathetic and more perfect than the Saviour; I say to myself with jealous love that not only is there no one else like Him, but there could be no one.'

Jesus is not a good way to heaven, He is the only way. The Bible teaches that heaven is not a reward, but a gift: 'For the wages of sin is death, but the gift of God is eternal life, through Jesus Christ the Lord.'[9]

So how then do we come to Jesus? How can we know that our sins are forgiven? How can we come to know God? How can we be sure of heaven when we die? The apostle Peter was asked similar questions. After preaching the first, great Christian sermon some weeks after Jesus had ascended to heaven, and the early Christians had received the Holy Spirit to live within them, Peter replied:

'Each of you must repent of your sins and turn to God, and be baptized in the name of Jesus Christ for the forgiveness of your sins. Then you will receive the gift of the Holy Spirit. This promise is to you, and to your children, and even to the Gentiles—all who have been called by the Lord our God.' Then Peter continued preaching for a long time, strongly urging all his listeners, 'Save yourselves from this crooked generation!'[10]

So, we are to turn from our sin, which is what the word 'repent' means, and to turn to God, which is believing. Then God gives us His Holy Spirit. In other words, we find that He has turned to us, and not only forgives all that is past, but comes to live within us, so that we become the temple of the living God. If this appears too easy, it is simply because the difficulty, the suffering, has already been borne by Jesus in His life, death and resurrection.

There are many encouraging passages in the Bible that teach this truth. Jesus said:

'For God loved the world so much that He gave His one and only Son, so that everyone who believes in Him will not perish but have eternal life. God sent His Son into the world not to judge the world, but to save the world through Him. There is no judgment against anyone who believes in Him. But anyone who does not believe in Him has already been judged for not believing in God's one and only Son. And the judgment is based on this fact: God's light came into the world, but people loved the darkness more than the light, for their actions were evil. All who do evil hate the light and refuse to go near it for fear their sins will be exposed. But those who do what is right come to the light so others can see that they are doing what God wants.'[11]

The apostle Paul wrote,

If you confess with your mouth that Jesus is Lord and believe in your heart that God raised Him from the dead, you will be saved. For it is by believing in your heart that you are made right with God, and it is by confessing with your mouth that you are saved. As the Scriptures tell us, 'Anyone who trusts in Him will never be disgraced.' Jew and Gentile are the same in this respect. They have the same Lord, who gives generously to all who call on Him. For 'Everyone who calls on the name of the Lord will be saved.' [12]

John, the disciple, wrote:

God showed how much he loved us by sending His one and only Son into the world so that we might have eternal life through Him. This is real love – not that we loved God, but that He loved us and sent His Son as a sacrifice to take away our sins. [13]

And at the very end of the Bible God sends out a final invitation to all people:

The Spirit and the bride say, 'Come.' Let anyone who hears this say, 'Come.' Let anyone who is thirsty come. Let anyone who desires drink freely from the water of life.[14]

Will you ask Jesus to be your Lord and Saviour today? With all my heart I encourage you to respond to God's love to you, by coming to the Lord Jesus, who is *the* way to God. You could pray this prayer:

O God, thank You that You know everything there is to know about me. I want to say that I am sorry for all my sin. With Your help I want to turn from it. Thank You for Your love toward me. Thank You that Jesus came into the world to live, and then die paying the penalty of all my wrongdoing. Thank You that He rose again from the dead. Right now, please forgive me. By Your Holy Spirit, come to live in my life. Please become my Lord, my Saviour and my Friend … forever. Help me to follow You and become more like You. Thank You for hearing this prayer, which I pray in the name of Jesus. Amen.

If you have prayed this prayer, it is just the beginning of your new life with Jesus. Please find a church which loves the Lord Jesus, believes the Bible and wants to introduce others to Him, and start to attend and get involved. Have a look at the www.tell-me-more.org website where you will find help in starting to grow as a Christian.

ENDNOTES

1. *Daily Telegraph*, 4th May, 2010.
2. Richard Bacon programme on 22nd November, 2007.
3. John 10:10.
4. John 14:6.
5. Acts 4:12.
6. 1 Timothy 2:5.
7. Luke 14:16-24
8. This is also the title of her autobiography, published by Fount in 1993. In 2010 she released a CD, 'What Wondrous Love Is This', produced by Manna Music.
9. Romans 6:23
10. Acts 2:38-40
11. John 3:16-21.
12. Romans 10:9-13.
13. 1 John 4:9 & 10.
14. Revelation 22:17.

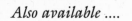

Also available ....

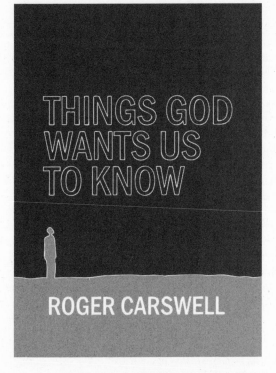

THINGS GOD
WANTS US
TO KNOW

ROGER CARSWELL

ISBN 978-1-84550-242-3

Things that God wants us to know

ROGER CARSWELL

Everybody has an opinion about God - but few people actually are brave enough to think it through. Thinking about God may result in changing things about your life! Many are prepared to share what they think about God but not so many have ever asked 'What does God want us to know about him?'. Here is just such a guide that distills the essence of the Christian message to those prepared to look for God.

Roger Carswell has spent many years explaining the Christian message to people, that experience comes through in this gift book that gently opens up a world of opportunities to those prepared to start thinking. Do you love someone enough to share the gospel with them. 'Things God wants you to know' will enable you to do this so that they can read it reflectively in their own time.

"These books are a wonderful tool for evangelism. We've bought a few boxes of Things God Wants You To Know *to use at our special events as a free give-away as people leave. They are affordable for the church, but most importantly they explain the gospel in such a clear and winsome way - we are delighted to be able to make this book available."*

Derek Guest ~ Vicar of St Andrew's Cheadle Hulme.

"...it is a lucid presentation of the gospel full of contemporary allusions, vivid illustrations and packs a powerful gospel punch. Open-minded friends would be pleased to be given this solid little book."

John Benton ~ Managing Editor, Evangelicals Now

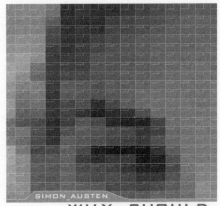

SIMON_AUSTEN

WHY_SHOULD
GOD_BOTHER
WĪTH_ME?

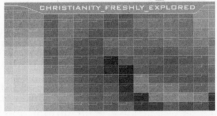

CHRISTIANITY_FRESHLY_EXPLORED

ISBN 978-1-85792-719-1

Why Should God Bother with Me?

Christianity Freshly Explored

SIMON AUSTEN

The modern secular viewpoint leaves us insignificant walking monkeys who got a lucky evolutionary break. NOTHING WE DO MATTERS. If you are investigating the Christian faith the question 'Why should God bother with me?' is one that needs an answer.

An accessible, engaging and comprehensive explanation of the Christian faith, which I thoroughly recommend.

Rico Tice ~ Author, Christianity Explored

Part C.S. Lewis, part John Stott, Austen invites conversation with unbelievers. God has in fact bothered with us more than we know.

Michael Horton ~ J. Gresham Machen Professor of Systematic Theology & Apologetics, Westminster Seminary in California, Escondido, California

If you are looking for a clear, straightforward explanation of the basics of Christian belief, in everyday language, this is your book. It is lucid, illuminating and very readable!

David Jackman ~ engages in a worldwide ministry for Proclamation Trust, London

Simon Austen has degrees in Science and Theology. A previous chaplain of Stowe School, he is now Vicar of Houghton and Kingmoor in Carlisle, England.

Christian Focus Publications

publishes books for all ages

Our mission statement –

STAYING FAITHFUL

In dependence upon God we seek to impact the world through literature faithful to His infallible Word, the Bible. Our aim is to ensure that the LORD Jesus Christ is presented as the only hope to obtain forgiveness of sin, live a useful life and look forward to heaven with Him.

REACHING OUT

Christ's last command requires us to reach out to our world with His gospel. We seek to help fulfil that by publishing books that point people towards Jesus and help them develop a Christ-like maturity. We aim to equip all levels of readers for life, work, ministry and mission.

Books in our adult range are published in three imprints.

Christian Focus contains popular works including biographies, commentaries, basic doctrine and Christian living. Our children's books are also published in this imprint.

Mentor focuses on books written at a level suitable for Bible College and seminary students, pastors, and other serious readers. The imprint includes commentaries, doctrinal studies, examination of current issues and church history.

Christian Heritage contains classic writings from the past.

Christian Focus Publications Ltd,
Geanies House, Fearn, Ross-shire,
IV20 1TW, Scotland, United Kingdom
info@christianfocus.com
www.christianfocus.com